Forever War

FOREVER WAR

YESYES BOOKS

Kate Gaskin

Cover art: *Woman Holding Brown Snake*
courtesy of Ck Lacandazo/Pexels.com
Author photograph © Dominic Gaskin

Cover & interior design: Olivia Croom Hammerman
Lead project editor: Stevie Edwards

ISBN: 978-1-936919-81-9

Library of Congress Cataloging-in-Publication data
available upon request.

Published by YesYes Books
1614 NE Alberta St
Portland, Oregon 97211
YesYesBooks.com

KMA Sullivan, Publisher
Stevie Edwards, Senior Editor, Book Development
Alban Fischer, Graphic Designer
Cole Hildebrand, Senior Editor of Operations
Amber Rambharose, Editor, Instagram
Alexis Smithers, Assistant Editor, *Vinyl* & YYB Facebook
Phillip B. Williams, Coeditor in Chief, *Vinyl*
Amie Zimmerman, Events Coordinator

For Dominic, all my love

Contents

What the War Was Not, What the War Was

I.

Letters, weeks filing past
between them, long-necked like vees

of geese. *Which outpost?*
Which outpost? You pouring sand

from your boots, your damp shirt
like another skin against

your skin. You didn't bring back
photos of the confetti

bombs made of the building's
rebar. I never had to imagine

the child's foot severed
in the roadway. You never flinched.

I didn't wait by the phone
for a year to catch

a few ten-minute calls tossed
like baseballs from across the sea.

2.

Omaha, in winter, like the ice
castles of Erhenrang, tunnels of snow
white   white

in the morning sun, the graveyard
beside our house   unmoored
headstones in a pale

body, undone. You somewhere
in Anbar swatting at flies
on the flight line. Just outside

the gate, a father
pushing his son in a wheelbarrow
the back of his head

just gone.

3.

I didn't receive your letters
sweetheart sweetheart

sweetheart. You didn't leave
me at the airport

on Valentine's Day. I didn't fall
and hit my head

on the toilet *baby's cries baby's cries*
or peer over hospital sheets

IV lines, our friends holding
our son. There was no mastitis, no

antibiotic regimen, no mammograms
no needles drawing fluid

from my breasts. You didn't call me
from beside a dumpster

in Al Udeid. You did not
tremble in the desert.

You did not beg
me to stay.

4.

I woke up on Bayou St. John
beneath the live oaks

and frisbees, the baby
asleep in his car seat. I nursed
in the cab

of my father's truck and read
your letters.

You said
you'd seen the inside
of a heart, the inside

of two cows, the red inside
of your eyelids

illuminated near-pink
those mornings in your tent
when sleep left you.

5.

There were no men
in service dress walking up

the front steps to our house
in Omaha, no house

no baby, no bedroom
lit blue from snow, no chilies

ground fine
in bowls. There was no

flag, no thirteen-fold, or sheep
skinned and drained

into buckets. You weren't
over a radio

tower in your plane
with no

ejection seat, no parachute
your radio radio. The streets

of the market
were not damp with blood.

The streets of the market
were not.

I. Home Front

In Which I Move Back in with My Parents

I wake
in my childhood bedroom. Outside
the backyard's dark

pines shiver. A county over
the Cahaba lilies are setting
the river on fire, and I

am thirty and home with an infant
alone. At the hospital
Tabitha, the receptionist, says *Girl*

how are you? And I
am seeing the breast specialist
about an abscess, a hole

the size of a baby's fist
and festering. There's Daisy
the ultrasound tech who touches me

so tenderly
I almost forget how popular she was—
white teeth, tan legs.

I've been away ten years, more
or less, and was happy to be gone
but now I'm back

in front of the mammogram machine
and this life, this life
is folding me in half.

Postpartum

Springtime, the azaleas
in bright flare, the baby there

beside the rocking chair
on my parents' front porch.

And you are where?
Here is a monotony

of baby gear, the swing
that clicks him side to side

a small origami
of laundry, loose bottles

frozen rings for his teeth
one breast that gives

its milk, and the other
that gives up in grief.

*

He is rolling over
front to back, back to front

as you crouch
in the desert and cradle

your phone. A miracle
to see it at all

from so many miles, the planes
that drone, the wind

that scabs the brush, your face
the crust of salt and dust

you wear like skin.
Again, you say. *Again.*

*

And tease me, my boots
my kin, the wind

in my hair down Elkahatchee
Creek, the shed skin

of ribbon snakes
in the summer when

we chased the low jewel
of Hale-Bopp

down our neighborhood streets.
I did not want to come home

to this, you gone, the ghost
of my legs whitening in the lake

you kissing me
you kissing me and then—

*

When you left
I dug myself up

like a bulb and moved
back home while you flew

off to war. Now I nurse
from my right side

as the catalpa trees
flush white

and the yard weeds over
in bright green.

Elegy with the Gulf of Mexico and the Persian Gulf

Here there is air same
as any other, twilight, sundog

haloing a different gulf
but water the same, sand

the same, same keening wind
same hollow in the body

scraped clean by loss. I am not
who I thought I would be

miraculously okay
with the difference between leaving

and being left. Wife
is a reductive word, gossamered

bereft, both passerine
and passive, the downy distance

between sky and ground. In war
all men are alike. They leave.

They go. Below: the sand, the water
the tide, this life I agreed to

even as I was being left behind.

After a While the Monsters

There were days
when trees pulled up their roots
curled in their leaves

whitened with blight and left
only dirt-churned ruts
dragging out from the yard.

All color paled from the crabgrass
and aphids left the garden
one by one. Even termites

ceased their endless chewing.
We threw bed sheets over the tables
blew out the candles,

rolled up the rugs and closed
the curtains against the night.
Tell me, when this is over

will all that's left for us to suffer
flee with winter?
Render itself toothless in the light?

Elegy with Citrus Greening and a 100-Year Flood

Whether trilliums appear
at the foot of March

or redbuds catch fire
and if cranes light

in the river or if bees
or morels beneath canopies

of hardwoods
or the Gulf licking up

into the hallways of pastel houses.
Even if elderberry

if oranges mottled and hard
in winter or the flit of kings

in their migration north
frozen in ryegrass

in the dead end of spring. Even then
even then in beauty

even if gone, if the water rising.

When All We Did Was Glitter

Those nights too
we went down the honeysuckle
road and picked

soft blossoms
their fragrance sweetening
our fingertips into petals

bright as the rising moon
and there in the dark
we pinched each tender throat

open, taking, because we could
and we were good
at it, all the nectar we wanted.

What did we know then
of the future throbbing outside
the delicate carapace

we made of that summer?
We just glowed and glowed
inside of it, so feverish, so gold.

Elegy with Whale Fluke and C-130s

The year I am born
the International Whaling Commission

decides *enough*
and ends commercial fishing

of whales, though who can legislate
the human heart's desire to name

and possess? The world was once rife
with baleen corseting and ivory-colored

cutlery handles, vast bobbing islands
of light fueled in the night

by whales. Now so few of them
are left. Good intentions

are sometimes worse. I know.
I have them every day, and yet

I order my time by listing
all I have to lose: child, bread, water

and whales, which are dying again
warming oceans emptying

of everything good as C-130s split
the sky above, heavy-bodied

and purposeful, so sure
there must be something left to save.

Ghazal for Alabama

And what of the river *Alabama*?
It is deep as the Coosa, the Cahaba, green as an Alabama

field—tall wiregrass, jade and then golden. In winter
the rye is green as the eyes of the first boy I loved in Alabama.

And in the pasture the hot tangle of pigweed is red
as a gummy smile, and the copperheads of Alabama

coil neatly in their soft nests of dead
leaves beneath the airy sycamores of Alabama.

And in the field there are bonfires and grain
alcohol and a pickup truck that peeled away into an Alabama

night—1995—a girl flung from the bed and paralyzed.
She never played her clarinet again in Alabama.

And later, two sisters in a rolled car in a peanut field
one calling her mother, the other lying in the soft Alabama

dirt, her leg wrong, her head wrong. She'll become so thin
and restless during the next decade in trailers across Alabama

like the trailer where Lacey lived with her two daughters
and husband. Where they smoked made-in-Alabama

meth and then left the girls alone to pick fields for stones
quartz and mica, anything with a little Alabama

shine until one day she wanted to stop, but her husband
didn't. He wanted to smoke all the meth in Alabama

beneath its simmering star-hot sky. This was before I left Alabama
for good. Some nights the moon was ripe as an Alabama

peach. Some nights I ate Chilton County peaches
over the sink in our first home in Alabama

as you pulled me closer, whispering *Kate*, and I knew you
loved me, you loved me, you loved me even more in Alabama.

Pennies

That summer was a man
gathering fury like weather
was a sweaty ring

on the railing was a lake
green with runoff
was a nest of banded

water snakes writhing
down a river was white
in the mouth

fat in the head was long
in the snout with heat-sensing
pits that summer

when we found blood
on the porch as if someone
were dragged from the door

a mating ball of garter
snakes in the yucca a headless
hen strung up from the oak

behind your father's house
where all that summer
we porch-sat and wished

on empties that glittered
the ditch across the street
as if they were pennies in a well.

Delta, Echo, Alpha, Romeo

January, Omaha splitting
open like a wound, like a moan
hard with teeth, back when

we spoke on the phone *delta, echo*
alpha, romeo all the tiny wicks
of dread curling their small

fires deep into my heart.
In Al Udeid, you said, the wind
in the sand was not quite

a lament, nor did your plane
mean certain death. Tell me
then, how you loaded

the bombs, how you parted
the air, how the ocean divides
breath between us. In Doha

you followed the sun
to the Gulf. Not once have I
believed we'll be spared.

II. Redeployment

Permanent Change of Station

I bought a little wooden house on a bay
and watched moon jellyfish throb
beneath the dock and out the other side
as you held the baby in your arms.

I watched moon jellyfish throb
upon the rock wall where they snagged themselves
as you held the baby in your arms
and turned to place your hand in mine

upon the rock wall where we snagged ourselves—
our marriage, the baby—and then you left
after you turned to place your hand in mine
in our house in Omaha. Outside snow was falling

on our marriage, the baby—and then you left.
Who says a military wife is strong?
In our house in Omaha, outside the snow was falling
and even in Qatar the sand was cold.

Who says a military wife is strong?
I fainted in the bathroom, dreamed of Florida
but even in Qatar the sand was cold
and you were gone for months and months

while I fainted in the bathroom, dreamed of Florida
held the baby to my breasts, and then, one day
when you were gone for months and months
I bought a little wooden house on a bay.

Monarch Season

Like any good thing, their days
are numbered, but here
in the October air, they're prolific

as if in the pulse-song of their pairings
they could carry us away.
I remember the fairytale of my first

true autumn, Omaha, the clear
dry air. Trees in their blazonry.
Sky bright and near. And you

in the glare over Hindu Kush
and then at a royal's house
Sea-Doos buzzing the cyan Gulf.

You brought home a five-foot tall
waterpipe, joked about when they
didn't have the cookies you liked

at the chow hall. Months of you
gone, then here, then gone
again, your plane a long

exposure spanning the Atlantic
from Nebraska to Qatar in one
blurry arc. We moved just when

your absences turned sour, and now
we live in the heartbeat of Monarch country.
They're endangered, you know.

They come and go
each fall, the air thick with their longing
to be anywhere but here.

The Exotics

What was it you said
    when the throng of gulls
        flocked to us like bed sheets

flung and pillowing
    as the sun disappeared
        into the white-flame sky?

All morning you beat back
    mimosas with your hatchet
        reclamation by the spit

of your sweat. A beat—
    and then they sprouted again.
        Don't tell the magnolias

about the dead hibiscus.
    They are already choked
        by an undergrowth viny

and damned. Love, I know
    we are penned in
        by an incomprehensible jungle.

Exotics fan their veins
    deep into the sand.
        But—look. From the wreckage

kudzu unfurls its delicate flower.
    Stingrays flit toward the mouth
        of the sea.

Fidelity

The former soldier occupies a threshold
between where his eyes meet mine

and where they're going, as if he thinks
I'm already a ghost, artillery smoke, a flare

shot over a river and receding. It's enough
to grab me by the knees, his short-cropped

hair, roughshod body that's had to shoulder
more than its fair share of sand flies

and trips outside the wire, but though I'm
tempted I don't make myself available

even when my heart—that salty-sweet hook
of mink and gravel—wants to.

What most men in this line of work long for
is a headful of hair like silk

to disappear into, arms like a May-sweet field
greening beneath the sun. Let these women

be simple as warm grass. Let them
be like gauze packing an open wound.

When my husband safely returns
he can't stop holding me. How easy it is

to be a cipher in my own story, incidental
and hollow, to have barely anything

to call my own. Even this keening desire
for more—I whistle it back. I call it home.

Bad Fruit

Say I come to you with an apple
for a palm. Would you eat it?

Perhaps the word etiquette
translated across a body of tenderness

becomes madness. If it is true
our bodies ripen and spoil

like fruit, then to capture the sweetest
bite is a trick. Say we marry

and our bodies become a road.
Day in and day out, we wind

past beautyberry, red basil, trees
with oranges like heavy yellow lungs.

In the yard is another fish-kill
and everywhere the oaks wear moss

for hair. I have heard
an unusual bounty of sharks

has been photographed beyond
the lip of the shore

and I have seen
the rough feast of dolphins

the brown curl of the tide
like a tendril of hair fallen

across the mouth of the sea.
We lost the hibiscus in the freeze

last winter. So many palm trees
have died on our watch.

Say I come to you with shoulders
like prickly pear and forearms

slick with pokeweed. For years I beg
you to eat. In the air ospreys sail

like a killing over small castles of fish.
When the sea rushes in

we pucker back our mouths and sputter.
What is saltier than two bodies in love?

Fuck, Marry, Kill

Definitely Marlon Brando, definitely biceps
white shirt, problematic

grease stains, definitely
longing and hot palmetto, rusted lacework

of wrought iron. Give me
a fantasy so humid I forget it's in black

and white. There are months when no one
touches me, months

of snow, the mailman trudging down sidewalks
hard-glazed with ice. In an email

I tell you I'd marry
Paul Newman, run away to his Connecticut

backyard, fortify my heart
with golden retrievers, salad dressing

a flame that never shakes. Tell me
what's at stake

in this war I can't hear or see? On the news
another woman explodes

in a crowded marketplace. Snipers go panther-
still behind their scopes. When you've been gone

long enough, I pour a glass of wine
and watch *Charade*. It's a big decision—who lives

who dies—but I'm lonely and I'm young
and this version of Cary Grant is done

for. When you finally come home, the thaw
slings up the tulips one by one.

Black Hawk

Multiple media outlets are reporting the cause of the March 10 Black Hawk
crash in the Santa Rosa Sound was the result of "spatial disorientation."

What they teach you
is that it takes only
thirty seconds for the ear
to come undone, and so
gravity unpicks its seams.

Checklist. Checklist.

My husband says you can prepare
years for this
and then in the space of seconds
three poor decisions release you
to the sky—or else

whatever's gone wrong
was already flinting in the machine's
belly before flight.

In any case, you will
never feel the spiral's grip
never see the closing credits
coming. Fog. Fog

which blurs and comforts
erases the membrane-thin shore.
What else could part heaven

from its reflection? What else
could soften the sound
from the sea?

Limnology

Even now—older—you are a lake
at daybreak, silver, feline, cranes

breaking the sylvan foot between trees
and waterline. You are the shore's

red mouth, mica glittering underfoot
the bass in the depths, the reeds

the snake in the reeds too. Between us
there is both drought and draught

years of thirst punctured with starbursts
of plenty, so much water I can barely

bring myself to breathe. Above
eagles, once gone, are arcing

from their eyries, swinging low to feed.
The water holds steady. Cold springs

bright teeth. Love
forgive my shallows. My endless need.

Sucker Hole

In the afternoons, thunderheads
spooled in from the sea. You used to joke

that from your office window
on base there was nothing but framed

clear sky, blue as the deep end of a pool
but on the flight line suddenly you were curtained

in by storms, fooled, once again, by a Florida
sucker hole. Each spring I watched dewberries

unwind in our backyard, counted wild shiso
wood sorrel, and chickweed too. You

resurrected the gardenia bush by the pergola
with just a bit of pruning, but I could lose

any planned thing to neglect, accidentally forget
a whole garden of tomatoes and crookneck

squash, the basil gone sour at the throat
of each leaf. Still, when our backyard

offered us wild berries in a brief
window of splendor, I took them. I watched

clouds pile against the planes over the bay
and each day you always came home.

III. Vietnam War

I.

You don't speak
much. There's drink
for that. A porch

to slick with chicken
blood, a rabbit's
foot, anything

to fold back the night's
eyelids, pin them
like moth wings

to the purple light
of morning. Each day
the same milk-warm

gestures. You knock
the dreams down
from the corners.

Air out the specters.
Chase off the batwing
felt of sleep.

2.

Outside My Tho
you said VC herded
children onto the road

shot anyone who tried
to save them, then shot
the children too.

I can show you
the exact tree that held
my brother's body

the lanyard of night
he slipped around his neck
but I've never heard

the cry of a gull.
What I am told of the sea
is that its waves

crest like bands
of running horses
that it's like a lake

of mountains, endless
and churned by beasts.
What I know of lakes

is personal, how I pale
bloodless in their grip
pecked occasionally

by fish, how flesh
is tendered
by water's slow embrace.

Who would I be
apart from these hills?
Beneath my fingernails

red crescents of mud
glow like embers
before moonrise.

In the dark, trails
spill from secret watchtowers.
Owls call from unseen

perches of night.
I can show you
what you don't want to see

a man hanging from a tree
a nest of water snakes
a beehive, every vine

of poison ivy winding
through this county.
One day my body

will be a bomb
going off in the street
but for now I will give you

small mercies—
two fawns, pearl-bright and hidden
in the sweetshrub

horses that crash
like waves
through the light.

3.

The fish—split and gutted—
jumped while limp in your hands
though it was far

from the river
and the dog whined from the forest
would no longer trail

your truck or enter the house.
Suddenly, you were clotted thick
with bug bites. Dark wet marks

bloomed like mouths
beneath your arms as the sun
made brittle paper of the leaves

as neighbors fell ill
for weeks and moths died one
by one against windowpanes

heaps of them quivering
in the morning wind, swirling
like ash from a fire.

The yard turned vacant
but for pigweed and tickseed.
The ivy's severed skeleton

tumbled its backbone
from the house.
What did you do, I said.

What happened to you?
But you only threw
the fish into the pan, clamped

the lid to hold it down
and you would not relent
to its suffering. These days

my heart is always tearing
away from itself
like a horse broken loose in a storm.

4.

Unwind the night's
ticking clocks—
feather, beak, claw

and eye. Loose
the snakes from the river
and curl them back

into the trees. Pick
the stars from the sky's
flat pitch, and snuff

the engine creaks
and whirs from the throat
of each unseen animal.

Unhear whatever happened
in the nearest, darkest tent
to the man with no clothes

no eyes, no tongue
no way to say he'd loved
no less than the men

holding fast the squares
of fabric to the ache
of his heaving mouth.

Unpour cup after cup
of water from the drowning
vessel of his face.

5.

The fields that fall
were honey and light
filtered through white

dove skies, a handful
of coyote holes, tracks
laid down by deer

and bobcats in the clay flats
by the stream, here
where you said you saw

you swear, a woman
on the rock bluff, naked
tied, and gagged.

Afterward, the flight back
and through the pasture
your mother out of breath

both of you parting
wiregrass and ragweed
running down the path

beneath the hickories
and no one there
not even the sedge

flattened from where
a body could have lain.
I believe you when you say

you saw children facedown
in the Mekong
how the water turned

blush at your boot tips
wind at your back
hot with dust and the taste

of iron rotting in your mouth.
If it proves anything
you can have me

by the swimming hole.
You can tie a rope
around my throat

and call me no better
than the stray
you found trembling

in a trash heap on the edge
of the ferny jungle.
If there was a woman

there, then we are
the same. Here
where rat snakes tunnel

the ryegrass
where purslane and ivy
come spilling

from the trees like red
gums through the night's bright
and whetted teeth.

6.

My love, I am not mad.
I know there are no elk in Alabama.
          I can't have seen it

but I have, standing
unbothered in the county road
          rack like a live oak
          rack like a car
its muzzle the color of a crow hopping down
                    bleached sedge in winter.

Must I remember
such things as they are? A thousand whitetails
flit through my dreams
                    but the elk, the elk
just stands.

*

Soon after, blood in the well.
                              Rust
some said
          but the water came up red.
I held my tongue forty days

and nights
forty raps to my hand with a ruler.

I sent up prayers
for horses in the field
and when the water cleared, I drew a big
clean breath, whispered the Apostle's Creed
to an empty pulpit.
This

of course, after I crushed
thirty-three eggs

in their nests
after I knocked the broom handle
on the barn door five times

five times a day

for five weeks. And the elk

it stood there
quietly.

Behind it, the barn in flames
wreathed by darting sparrows.

*

I have had a premonition.
A field shorn for winter, a hundred

                        fawn-colored bucks
throats slit and blackening the grass.

            The blank witness of the sky
            like a mouth slackened in sleep
            and at the edges, dark pines

whispering what they had seen
in a language I'll never know.

*

                        At your request
I said I never saw it, brown and real
            as a dog, quiet as any doe

grazing in the backyard.

And yet I had
coming back from town
beautyberry spilling from the shoulders
as if to pave the road
the deep violet of the sea.

                              I'd seen its eyes
their oval pupils, thick slash
of eyelashes, female in excess.

My heart became wings beating
                              blood to my ears.

Rustling in the eaves

sparrows lit
in pairs to their nests

in the barn before it burned.

*

And their song
                    which has fallen silent
before October's combines
hay, and clay red as the body

as the underside of the carcass
strung up and cooling

           above the bucket
                       in our yard.

7.

Twilight of mud
and gleaming, the snakes
plop like hands

to the river's brown mouth.
In the bucket a bullfrog.
In the bucket a ruin

of earth twisting with worms.
You tell me to listen
for footsteps, a horned crown

that slides between pines.
Hooves, you say, are fingernails
packed into a cloven point.

At night you murmur
a kicked bees' nest
sweat through piles

of thick afghans, darken
the room with just your breath.
Whatever's after you

will soon be after me.
You say come
and take me down

a black moon path
my feet two snuffling snouts.
The forest closes.

I know that possums
hang like fruit
from all the trees.

8.

I feel them everywhere
whittling me bone-thin
with serrated teeth.

In the dark, a man sings
to his guitar, one note
cutting ragged

from his throat. Earlier
we touched each pebble
on the path. Our faces

filled up like ticks. Our hair
grew coarse as batwings.
We flew with our treasures

into caves and sorted
through them there—
rusted pull-tabs, yellowed

straws, a cigarette
butt marked by a perfect
kiss, and bits

of glass so fine
I thought they'd turn
to powder in our hands.

All this, and still we picked
at bugs we could not
see. We came

undone like rolls
of parchment. Someone
had untied our string.

What is home? We soon
made suffering from it.
When we left, we didn't

miss our couches.
When we left, we didn't
mourn the phone.

We left it flatlining
on the floor, and no one
stopped to lock the door.

9.

You said
it was a different time.
The sun was a room

with a locked door, and all the black
eyes of the jungle
followed you from hut to hut

beneath alien constellations
of light. Even now
from time to time

the sky closes its lid like a trunk
and rain falls up from the ground
and worms thread down

all around you
from the mouths of starlings
melting back

into the night. But for now
you wake, here, in the soft
palm of our bedroom

your dreams grim as vultures
eyeing the shoulders
of any dark road leading home.

10.

Why are there only
two wars in this book
there is never not a war

somewhere the one
we were born into and
the legacy we'll leave our son

like sun shot through
elephant grass eucalyptus
trees crosshatching

the moon there is never not
a bullet longing
for a heart to enter

and possess never
an explosion that doesn't
yearn to claim the pink mist

of ravens a snake a pair
of legs that just yesterday
were laced tight

with muscle and loved
by someone I'm telling you
there is never not a woman

waiting never an after
never a before
this very moment our child

skipping through a room
without you and lifting his finger
like a pistol *boom*   *boom*

IV. Forever War

Forever War

Because we can be undone
by routine violence
because you call this conflict

the forever war, because history
is a needle quilting itself
to the same thirsty bedrock

my white ancestors claimed
there is only, in the end, the matter
of our shared complicity.

I am no better
with no finger on a trigger
than any other colonizer, and you

with your immigrant mother
and the bombs you loaded
onto Jeannie Leavitt's plane

are only one man among many
telling the same lie: that air power
can suture the musculature of war

shut for good. Can this ever
be undone? Now drones. Now the same
Groundhog Day of special ops

humping across dry lands
most Americans could never name.
You are gone

in your plane over the Tigris
again, and here there is only Nebraska
and wind, my insufficient

hands, the dumb and bloody language
of the tongue I cannot shed.

After the Surge

In class the professor pairs me
with a former soldier
who has been *over there*

thinking we share
a kind of common affliction.
He will not look at me.

He will only look ahead.
At home I am another soldier's wife
a portal—bone-colored—back

to the original wound, a rib
wet and steaming he cradles
in his hands. Let me be

like a man. Let me stand at the edge
of any ocean. Let me swallow
the swells of black water.

I will eat the air
the brackish ships rowing in
and I will never have my fill.

Elegy with Altitude and Skyscrapers—
Al Udeid Air Base, Qatar

Having never been to war myself
I can only read about it

in your emails. The boredom.
The cold. Candy bars and long hours

in a plane over frozen mountains
far above the explosions, the woven

rugs, hot tea in cups. We make
inhuman whatever we can

for our own good. To forget. To sleep
finally in our beds at night. Your quarters

are close. Your conversations
with your buddies always turn back

to women, how they leave. Even
the commanders' wives eventually

gather their children
like scarves and coats at the end

of a long night. There are casualties
for every airstrike. So much rubble

beneath the rubble we'll never
quite reach its end. Is your favorite

kind of ice cream at the chow hall?
Will you walk through gleaming Doha

in the morning? On base you run
a 10K in the dark and write *I love*

I love I love you. In the city
beyond the gate, an opulence of palms

and glass towers glistens. To see it
you'd never guess what we have done.

Retrieving the Guns

I.

When you leave for the third time
I drink pink wine and shuffle along

the hall we painted orange, a color
to keep us warm. I sing

I don't know how to love him, and I
really lean into it, this pain

that comes with each departure, bright
and clear as a sudden bruise.

Before your first deployment
you spent about a year

training. When you weren't flying
you wandered the squadron

searching for a place to sit. Each day
the corn grew taller in its fields.

You emptied
the trash, and you waited.

2.

Part of your love for me
is formed from the same impulse

you have to sprint to a burning car.
Just like your ex-wife's

need for you, my need
for you gives you something

to shovel towards. When you leave
I sit in our dusk-gutted house

and wait for night. You write
Send my jacket, please. The desert

is cold. Years later, when we
have better phones, you strain

for a signal, crouch on your heels
by an Al Udeid dumpster. Winter

in Omaha is cruel as a trap
I gnaw at each day. *Please come home.*

3.

It's April. You're in civilian clothes
at a Qatari prince's mansion

on the Persian Gulf, and there are Sea-Doos.
Is this war too? I can't imagine you

in swim trunks, can't see anything
but your tan flight suits, your stiff blue

PT gear, but when you packed, you must have
included slacks and a button-down

shirt for trips into Doha. You buy
a hookah downtown and ship it back

to the States. You write, *Some nights
there's nothing to do but read books*

*in my bed. Some days there's nothing
but sea.*

4.

Monday nights after class
I go with Dora and Scott

to the Homy Inn where there are peanuts
in dog bowls and pitchers

of champagne on tap. The echo
of cigarette smoke perfumes

the whole room, and if
I strain I can be

just a normal 26-year-old eating oranges
from pints of Blue Moon.

5.

When I met you, you were already
six years enlisted. You

were my winter boyfriend, but when the time came
to break up, we moved

to Texas instead. Nights I couldn't sleep
I woke you just to touch you

as the strip club next door flushed
our apartment pink. We were married

in the Garden for the Blind.

6.

Every day there are more deaths
reported. We exchange emails. You write

They didn't have peanut butter cookies
at the chow hall today. War

is hell. I picture you
in the sky, the refueling jet twinned

to your plane. You over the radio, over
Anbar, over a burning village with high

concrete walls. You eat beef jerky
and Snickers bars, cash in your three

drink tickets after debriefings
sleep well past the dawn. Smoking hookah

with Dora, I drop embers
and they incandesce in a sudden bright

crown. Sometimes this city feels like light
in my mouth. On the news

another helicopter is down.

7.

Before the initial invasion
the small college where we met

hosted a pro-war rally. You walked
stunned through the posters

and chants. I was not your wife yet
and the dead still had

their warm bright hearts
beating like wings in their chests.

8.

In the auditorium the base commander
addresses the wives, saying, *Here we value*

faith first, and then family, and then freedom.
Faith: the black limbs of elms bowing

under snow, Omaha in January, the air
so bracing it steals itself back

from my lungs. *Family:* Dora at the Waiting
Room Lounge, whiskey and 7-Up

and too much fun, Sheila says, or so
she's heard, her eyes big, bovine

with concern. *Freedom:* summer, a river
your hands. Rewinding

the tape past each explosion.
Retrieving the guns from the men.

9.

The thread that connects us
golden and thin

from the fist clenching me
in the middle of my country

to the dunes of sand
that rise like waves

around yours, is the relief
we share that, for you, war

is something that happens
in the black currents of air

over the Persian Gulf or Hindu
Kush, high above the Humvees

and roadside bombs and calls
to prayer.

10.

Your first job was loading bombs
onto Strike Eagles. There are photos of you

on the flight line in your coveralls
in wind, in snow and sleet, on days

so hot you iced yourself in the bath
after your shift ended. When you enlisted

it was still the '90s, and airmen could go
a whole career deploying once, maybe

twice. Now, you're home for a handful
of weeks before you leave again, and this

is what you know: that your first marriage
is to the sky, that one wife left

and the other stayed, that it is better
to die in a spiral dive, your inner ear

bobbing obliviously
as the plane falls like a winged seed.

Elegy with Snow and Dying Maples

Lately, ice-limned branches
perch in threat over
power lines. The hardtack

of snow is beaten slick
into the walkway. Even my breath
hangs itself in a pale afterlife

that issues from the only warm
body left in our house.
Lately, I can't stand a damn

thing. I would never choose
a winter like this. And I curse it
all. The air itself, the grackles

in their evening grouse
as they rattle century-old
maples that, planted all at once

are now dying, buckling
under winter's lead apron
of ice as if executed one by one

by the snow. Once, I asked you
to explain the difference
between mortar and mortar

rounds, and you said one
is the instrument and the other
a bomb good for lobbing

over high village walls.
There are no explosions here
only people shrugging

into the cold. The radio tallies
the dead as your plane
grazes over their cities, and when

a branch falls in our backyard
suddenly in a shock
of sound, it unveils a new heart

of blue sky where once
there was just tree, and a fine cloud
of snow, like ash, settling.

What Will Come to Pass

In the future, water will meet sky
until each pale-faced house drowns

beneath the mirror of itself. Roaches
will huddle in the bottoms of empty boats

and blooms of jellyfish will boil the sea.
Do you remember the little yard, eaten

by clover and wisteria? How when thickets
of conradina flowered, their buds opened

into tiny hearts like purple rooms with purple
tongues that beat into our hands? Let us say

we'll stay in the palm of this gray world
just this once okay with the risen water

at peace with what we have to lose, fanning
open branches from the forest, releasing

the bottle-blue hours, the sun upon us
like a warm egg breaking open into yolk.

Elegy with Sunset and a Cautionary Tale

We have learned to count the last days of summer
by the arrival of the catamaran perched like an ibis

in the blue stretch of bay just beyond the no wake
marker, bobbing there for days in its crisp seersucker

its whiff of sunscreen, wad of damp towels, a cabin
table sticky with rum. At sunset, the neighbor's grandsons

run shrieking down his dock, holding aloft sparklers
in the winking light, the horizon like a bowl of Rainier

cherries a day gone from rot. I scrub spaghetti sauce
from the floor, squat before the cat litter, stand weakly

in the bathroom doorframe at the last wash of light.
How many days have I wished to have back

until I've unwished them all, rending us
like a zipper's popped mouth, our airless lungs gasping?

Aftermath

In November I dreamed you left again
and like an improbable rain

babies began falling. Bouncing
unharmed like marshmallows

they landed between the marshland
and river. In a stand of scrub oaks

with banks edged in goldenrod
herons slipped seamlessly between

the blanks of their secret paths.
Above, dark birds assembled

in constellations, first Rorschach
blots, then ribbons of smoke coiling

into the sky. For months we weathered
a drone of unstoppable tides

winnowing, winnowing, each of us
etching into a collection of teeth

and fine bones, our stomachs like shells
curling inward, pink and cochlear.

Only the popped mouths of stranded
muscles sustained us. When I woke

I was reaching for them, into the warm
curve of your back. Once you left

you never stopped leaving.
Do you understand that?

The Foxes

They came like emissaries
from a fairy tale. In twilight, framed

by wisteria vines that burdened
the backyard's power lines, they dozed

like cats all summer. Awake
they tussled up and down the honeysuckle

still kits, all muzzle, light feet.
This was years after one of your troops

froze to death on the concrete staircase
outside his Florida apartment.

Years after you loaded your last
bomb. Years of desert deployments.

And now this house, its kind porch
and open rooms, the foxes we inherited.

Though eventually they too left
and the sickness that follows us took root.

Wherever we go, these black blossoms.

Operations Suite

I let myself believe
we retired your desert

flight suit, shipped it, chastened
back to 2007 when your plane

was a neon thundering that split
the tropopause

*

in two. Those first few
weeks without you, the baby's

black eyes staring up
from the crook of my arm

while snow fell through
the elms. I too

*

am distrustful of any group
in lockstep—large

manipulations of starlings
formations of them

on the parade
ground, *reveille, reveille,* and yet

*

if a plane is just a ribcage falling
then a man is just a ribcage begging

*

over Kandahar. Your voice
tinny and small, ricocheting

off glinting satellites
back to me. In those days

I could never drink so much
as a whiskey without trying

to replace myself entirely

*

with another   kind   of woman

one   who wouldn't   wait

*

for you through thunder
that growled

from the margins of the woods
as I stood

ankle-deep in a flood
the doves promising your return

like clockwork
back to the bougainvillea

each spring. You can

*

lie to me this time—say
you'll stay. Hindu Kush

rising from the horizon
like rows of frozen teeth.

Notes

"Ghazal for Alabama" is after Bruce Snider's "Map." This poem is for Brooke Ethridge.

The title "Permanent Change of Station" refers to the military term for receiving orders to relocate to a new duty station.

The epigraph in "Black Hawk" is from the *Pensacola News Journal* article "Reports: Cause of Black Hawk Crash Released."

"Unwind the night's" is after Ansel Elkins's "Reverse: A Lynching."

"Why is there only" is for Christina Olson.

In "Forever War" Jeannie Leavitt was the U.S. Air Force's first female fighter pilot.

"Retrieving the Guns" borrows a line from *Jesus Christ Superstar*: "I don't know how to love him."

Acknowledgments

Thank you to the editors of the following journals for publishing these poems, sometimes in different forms.

Alaska Quarterly Review: "Ghazal for Alabama" and "Fidelity"

Bellevue Literary Review: "Aftermath"

Blackbird: "In Which I Move Back in with My Parents," "Delta, Echo, Alpha, Romeo," and "Operations Suit"

Cherry Tree: "The Exotics" and "Elegy with Altitude and Skyscrapers"

Cimarron Review: "Bad Fruit"

The Florida Review: "Twilight of mud"

The Fourth River: "Monarch Season" and "What Will Come to Pass"

Guernica: "Cousin, I am not mad"

JuxtaProse: "After a While the Monsters"

Ninth Letter Web Edition: "When All We Did Was Glitter" and "You don't speak"

Passages North: "Fuck, Marry, Kill" and "Elegy with Snow and Dying Maples"

The Pinch: "What the War Was Not, What the War Was"

Poetry Northwest: "The Foxes"

Puerto del Sol: "Pennies"

Radar Poetry: "Outside My Tho" and "The fields that fall"

Raleigh Review: "I feel them everywhere"

The Rumpus: "Sucker Hole," "Limnology," and "Forever War"

Sixth Finch: "Elegy with Whale Fluke and C-130s"

storySouth: "Permanent Change of Station"
Sugar House Review: "Black Hawk"
Tar River Poetry: "Elegy with Sunset and a Cautionary Tale"
Thalia: "Unwind the night's"
THRUSH: "Elegy with Citrus Greening and a 100-Year Flood"
Tinderbox Poetry Journal: "The fish, split and gutted"
War, Literature and the Arts: "Postpartum"
Whiskey Island: "You said"

Thank you to KMA Sullivan and Stevie Edwards for believing in *Forever War* and giving it a home. Thank you to Stevie, especially, for your guidance, support, and expertise. I have endless gratitude for the entire angelic staff at YesYes Books. Thanks for everything y'all do.

Thank you to Mel Oliveira for agreeing to read my work all these years and for letting me return the favor. Thank you to Christina Olson for the invaluable gift of helping me see the true order of this book, as well as volunteering your time to help me grow as a poet. Thank you to Sydney Wade for some practical, much-needed line edits when I had no one else to ask. Thank you to Amorak Huey for choosing "What the War Was Not, What the War Was" for *The Pinch's* 2017 Literary Award in Poetry, an honor that helped me feel seen. Thank you to Colby Cotton for helping me see what needed to be left out. I'm indebted to Jehanne Dubrow for generously writing a thoughtful blurb for *Forever War*. I'm also grateful to AWP's

Writer to Writer mentorship program, as well as the Sewanee Writers' Conference, for the gift of community and guidance.

Thank you to my parents for being proud of me. To Connie Ralston—thank you for modeling, from the very beginning, what being a reader and writer and lover of poetry looks like. Finally, thank you to Dominic, without whom this book would not exist. Your limitless support of and belief in me make all this possible. I love you.

Kate Gaskin's poems have appeared in journals such as *Guernica, Pleiades, Poetry Northwest, 32 Poems, Alaska Quarterly Review, Tin House, The Southern Review, The Rumpus,* and *Blackbird,* and her work has been anthologized in the *2019 Best American Nonrequired Reading.* She is a recipient of a Tennessee Williams Scholarship from the Sewanee Writers' Conference, as well as a fellowship from the Vermont Studio Center. In 2017 she won *The Pinch's* Literary Award in Poetry. *Forever War* is her first book of poems.

ALSO FROM YESYES BOOKS

Fiction
Girls Like Me by Nina Packebush

Recent Full-length Collections
Ugly Music by Diannely Antigua
To Know Crush by Jennifer Jackson Berry
Gutter by Lauren Brazeal
What Runs Over by Kayleb Rae Candrilli
This, Sisyphus by Brandon Courtney
Salt Body Shimmer by Aricka Foreman
Ceremony of Sand by Rodney Gomez
Undoll by Tanya Grae
Everything Breaking / For Good by Matt Hart
Sons of Achilles by Nabila Lovelace
Landscape with Sex and Violence by Lynn Melnick
GOOD MORNING AMERICA I AM HUNGRY AND ON FIRE
by jamie mortara
Stay by Tanya Olson
a falling knife has no handle by Emily O'Neill
One God at a Time by Meghan Privitello
I'm So Fine: A List of Famous Men & What I Had On by Khadijah Queen
If the Future Is a Fetish by Sarah Sgro
Gilt by Raena Shirali
Boat Burned by Kelly Grace Thomas
Helen Or My Hunger by Gale Marie Thompson

Recent Chapbook Collections

Vinyl 45 s

Exit Pastoral by Aidan Forster
Of Darkness and Tumbling by Mónica Gomery
The Porch (As Sanctuary) by Jae Nichelle
Juned by Jenn Marie Nunes
Unmonstrous by John Allen Taylor
Preparing the Body by Norma Liliana Valdez
Giantess by Emily Vizzo

Blue Note Editions

Beastgirl & Other Origin Myths by Elizabeth Acevedo
Kissing Caskets by Mahogany L. Browne
One Above One Below: Positions & Lamentations by Gala Mukomolova

Companion Series

Inadequate Grave by Brandon Courtney
The Rest of the Body by Jay Deshpande